The Best of Shirl's Words

Poems from Life

Shirley Richards

ISBN 978-0-06450417-0-5

Author Photography: Kerry Bethune

penneywrites@gmail.com

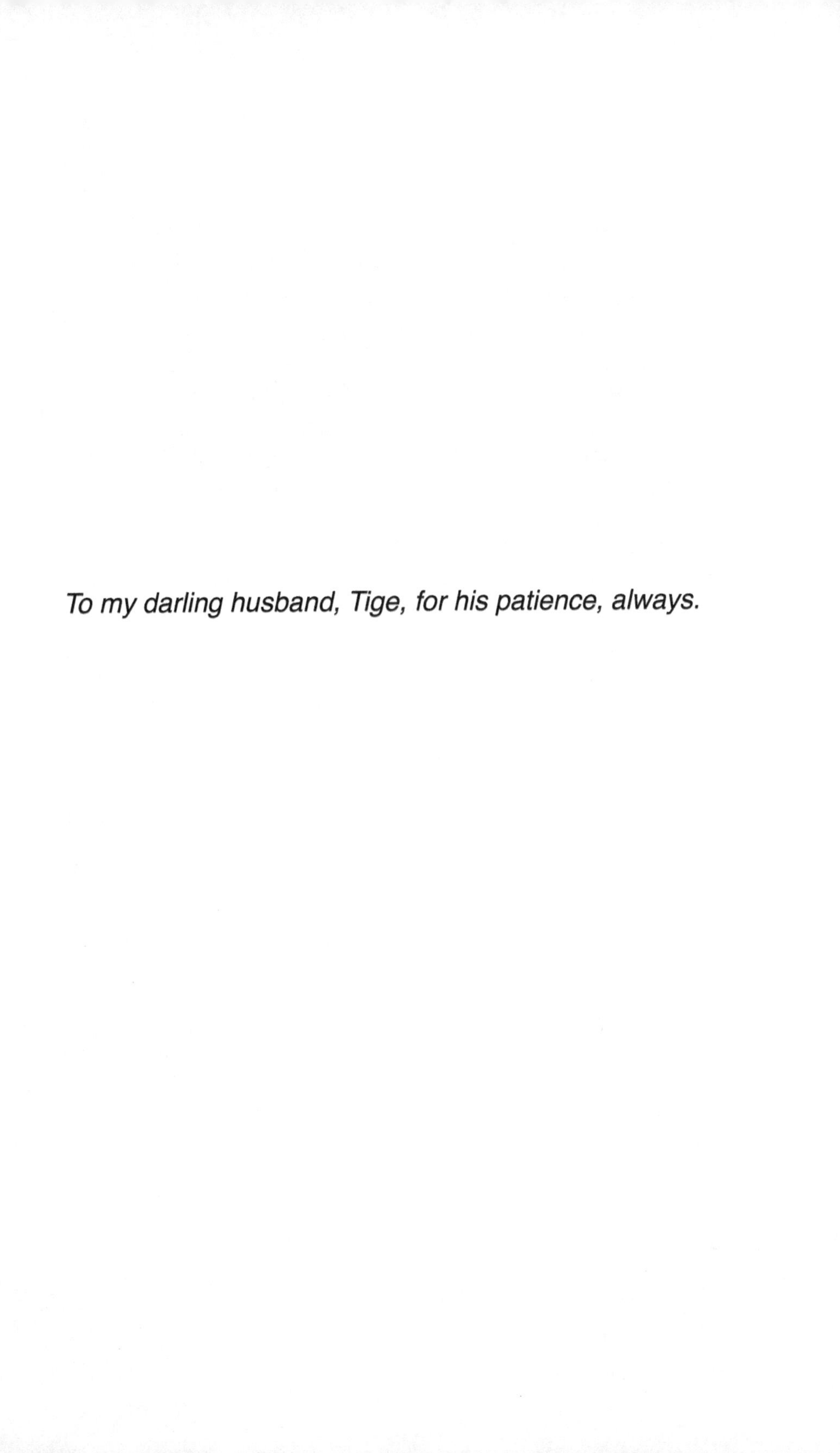

To my darling husband, Tige, for his patience, always.

Shirley

Being named Shirley makes you happy and bright
For it comes from Yorkshire, an English delight.
It was first a place name then later a surname
And mid-19th century it hailed as a boy's name.
It means 'shire and meadow', outgoing and free
And came in to fame via author Charlotte Bronte
From her heroine 'Shirley' who overthrew strife
And urged women to seek wider choices in life.
Her name is synonymous with a free-thinking girl
And has a pet name now abbreviated to Shirl.
Whilst in the 1930s Shirley Temple, child star,
Revived the name and made it most popular.

Butterflies Are Free

Butterflies are free
As should all poets be
To soar, to dream, to contemplate
All notions and word pictures make.
Butterflies are free
Wings kissed by the softest breeze
To fly aloft to flap on by
About the southern clear blue sky.
And, when a sonnet new, is born
Inspired from the early whisps of dawn
Out of a jewelled emerald sea,
A poetic metamorphosis begins -
Setting poets, like butterflies, free!

Robots, Drones and Frankenstein

Nearly 200 years ago
There was a hue and a cry –
Mary Shelley penned a monster:
Dr Frankenstein's unreal guy!
Today they've created robots
And drones that literally fly,
An inventor's gifted foresight
Programmed via computer wi-fi.
Online Santa's new mates -
Also known as 'bots and drones
Relieved the elves' work loads
Sorting new iPads and iPhones
The world's in automotive mode
Android Santa has auto-load
For online - buy was at his door
Making real-time shop a less chore
Swifter was this modern system
Pick and pay, press and send
Purchases arrived at your door
Drone-delivered for your spend.
If Frankie's monster trod earth today,
He'd lose his bolts to ride the sleigh
With mini-monsters stowed away
While robotic-deer sled the Milky-Way!

The Voice

The marriage of voice and words
Waxed lyrical over the early birds.
A random dip into the mail sent in
Kept the larynx taut and vocals trim.
John Reid recited topics in rhyme
As his listeners hung on every line,
With cups and saucers rattling so,
Biscuit dunkers enjoyed the show.
Unusual was the time and place
Yet it put a smile on many a face
To hear their words read on radio
At the crack of dawn on ABC 3LO.
The years slipped by so readily
And as John read words steadily
A plot had been slowly galvanised
Which left his listeners so surprised!
The show was axed no more to be
It was a shock none could foresee
Then like a Phoenix rising up again
Friends of ABC Poets' Corner came.
For 22 years following John's theme
People united to keep up, the dream
The poets were writing topics to print
In the quarterly newsletter's new link.
The era is over a second time round.
Time will tell if there'll be a new ground.
The rhythm of verse is a powerful thing
And is food for thought in resurrecting.

The Teabag Blues

The cast aside ol' teapot,
used to be sought after,
Once graced the finest tables,
of knights and kings like Arthur.
How the ladies loved it,
such a fuss they'd make,
With lace cloth on the table,
best china cup and plate.
Set about so orderly for everyone to see.
Their dainty fingers poised
so, as they sipped their tea.
But alas, that's all gone now,
since teabag made the scene.
The teapot just gets dust on it,
or is very rarely seen.
Though handy when you're busy,
as modern folk you see
Can't spare the time with working,
to fuss when making tea.
They use a thing tied to a string,
and jiggle it up and down,
Or (maybe) throw it in a teapot
and hope it doesn't drown.
Now teabags are so handy,
for plain jiggling around,
But, teapots and fine china,
make a lovely clinking sound...
So, to anybody out there,
who feels the same as me
And loves a good ol' cuppa,
then here's the recipe...

THE RECIPE… Boil kettle, rinse out teapot With hot water,
Add one teaspoon of tea leaves for each person and one

for the pot, Pour in boiling water, allow to brew a minute, turn the teapot three times, then pour into china cups for the best results.

 (Included in a collection of poems held by the Twining Tea Company, London, England.)

Australia Day

As we celebrate Australia's birthday
I thank my lucky star
For being born an Aussie
In the land that's best by far.
For her skirt of clear blue water
That sweeps our big brown land,
Where kangaroo and emu roam
Within her outback span.
For her leafy-green umbrellas
Casting their shadows far and wide
O'er dale and rocky summit
Where Snowy Mountain Horsemen ride.
For her rustic cattle stations
Where 'Hele-Cowboys' glide,
Mustering up wild horses
O'er the sunburnt country-side.
For her long white sandy beaches
And rivers snaking-wide,
For tall gum trees where koalas chew,
In AUSTRALIA lives my pride!

City Daze

Daily pushing through their paces
Pain rides over people's faces
No-one smiles much in the city
There's much indifference, more's the pity.
People look - but do they see
The buskers busking busily,
Or the clever footpath artist's chalk
Erasing slowly as past they walk?
Ribbon development - wall to wall
Concrete snaking the buildings tall
Bustling people on a shopping bent
Bodies aching and their credit spent.
Tho' it's a fact that city fellers
Love their lives as city dwellers.
Their country cousins often reel
From swollen ankles or a blistered heel.
There're theatres plush with comfy seats
Where audiences applaud the actors' feats.
And people-queues, bag jugglers all,
Where ankle-biters start to bawl.
Cities are curious conurbations
Designed to titillate imaginations,
And while the city seems to sleep
Robots give grit and grime a sweep.

Life in the Slow Lane

Being a tortoise would be oh, so cool,
Moving in the slow lane that is the rule.
Armour plated against elements and foes
Carting its carapace wherever it goes.
Keeping upright is of paramount order
For a tortoise is oval rather than broader.
Giants live to be one hundred and fifty,
Life in the slow lane would be oh, so nifty.
Tho' comical looking on its quadruped feet,
The in-shell tortoise is really quite complete.
It can play dead and any of its predators foil
Or escape bushfires by burrowing into the soil.
I'm in awe of the tortoise's Herculean size,
And its reptilian head and bright beady eyes,
Its tile-like shell and its jack-in-a-box nape
And for being nicer than a slithering snake!

A Matching Pair

The button jar was overflowing
A stow of discs awaited sewing.
Deft fingers acted with rapid speed,
For thread and needle were in need.
Through generations, four, I've been,
From Great Grandma Geraldine,
To Granny Lil of London Town
She hugged me tight as bombs fell down.
When Nanna Rae was just a child,
She acted rash, she cared wild,
She dropped me in the toilet bowl
And tried to flush me down the hole.
Then as she hung me out to dry
She noticed I had lost an eye.
So buttonless in a covered box I lay
Till a new grandchild was on the way.
When mother-to-be had finished sorting
Bright button eyes I soon was sporting.
For the button jar held a matching pair…
Now I'm reinstated as the nursery bear!

He Loves Me - He Loves Me Not

He loves me when
I sing off key.
He loves me when
I recite poetry.
He loves me when
I'm running late.
He loves me when
I make him wait.
He loves me when
I'm out of gasoline.
He loves me when
I'm acting mean.
He loves me when
I take the biggest
Piece of cake.
He loves me when
I'm grossly overweight.
He loves me when
I pull out plants,
Instead of weeds.
He loves me when
I cast his fishing-line
Into the reeds.
He loves me when
I burn the toast.
He loves me when
I overcook the roast.
He loves me-not... when
I touch his restored MORRIS MINOR
Guess what?
He loves me!

True Love Blooms

My secateured hand
Hovers - bee-like.
The severed stem bleeds
Like an open wound.
Cool water soothes
In crystal.
A sweet scent permeates
The room.
The deep red strikes me -
Like shot arrows from
Cupid's bow.
'Better than Chanel'
YOU SAY.
Slowly turning,
I face an empty room.
Thru' moist eyes -
A plethora of roses
Appear
Yours.
Grown from bud to bloom
True love abounds.

Head Song O' Love

A call rang out
From a peaceful dove
Winged on a dream
Of a yesterday love.
Heady and beguiling
The love bird sang
With notes scintillating
A doo-del-oo rang.
Backcombing the years
Two sweethearts cried
Of a first love thwarted
Their young hopes denied.
Beyond love's bitter-sweet mire
There's a melody bird
That mends broken hearts
When her loves song is heard!

Nevermore Come!

Nevermore come, yesterday,
It's gone and out of sight.
Nevermore come, yesterday,
Tho' I wish it with all my might.
Nevermore come, yesterday,
Time travellers on its way,
And a new day is birthing
With the given name: Today.
Today will vanish all too soon
When night is on the run,
To be swallowed up by the dawn
And smirched by the rising sun.
Tomorrow is so far away,
The future yet unclear,
And after living thru' today
The 'morrow nudges near.
Amassing many yesterdays
Between three score and ten,
I fold them into memories
For they'll nevermore come again!

The Model

I hate that model's stride and bound
Parading up and parading down,
On stiletto heels she struts her stuff,
So pencil thin, with hair of fluff.
She flaunts her body and sways her hips,
Veneers her hair and glosses her lips.
Her face it wears a painted smile,
She peacocks clothes there in the aisle.
I hate that model's stride and bound
Parading up and parading down,
On a cat-walk made for mannequins
Wearing designer clothes with expensive trims;
And how she shakes her derrière
And tosses her head with a pretentious air
And pirouettes off, on ankles fine,
With a chassis that's not a bit like mine!

A Wordy Appetite

In fits and starts it haunts me
Neither constant nor grammatically
Gnawing deep within my brain
It won't let up - tho' I don't complain
There stirs a spark of imagination
Brought about via an observation,
Nourished on the material at hand.
The sky, the sea, the golden sand.
Swallowed up and then digested
Thought about and orally tested.
When inspiration's on the boil
My faculties must mull and toil.
For short the muses often live
When creative juices flow and sieve.
Rotund or slim in shape or size
I mould and mix to make a prize.
I turn a phrase, whip up a theme
At first a notion kicks in keen,
Then wanes and dies on centre stage
Or simply runs right off the page.
Two plus five the drafts can be
Before the lines hold symmetry.
When suddenly, there's food for thought...
A wordy appetite's been caught!

Teardrops of Joy

Joyful teardrops fall on lace
And trickle down a jaunty face.
A lifted veil, handled with care,
Finds sparkling eyes hiding there.
'Kiss your bride,' the minister said:
'For you are now truly wed!'
A nervous groom eagerly complied
Kissing happy teardrops aside.
The present time deleting pain
For life anew they did reclaim
Trusting happiness to abide,
All teardrops wiped away and dried.
At last, today they walk as one
Approved by carers barring none.
To live together on the sunny side
Of the nursing home where they'll reside.

A Hole in One

Statue-like with legs aplenty
In possum pose ready to fight
A tawny shape catches my eyes
I freeze at this ghastly sight.
It hugs the bench in our garage,
My mind boggles at its awesome size.
Gingerly I address a shifty plan
A fail-proof one on its demise.
I count the ways to slay the brute:
Knock it down. Swat it with a broom.
Douse it well with a deadly spray,
And put it in a permanent swoon.
Instead, I muster him from indoors:
Darling, bring along your old golf stick,
There's a huntsman lurking in the shed.
I trust you can erase it fairly quick?
My hero sizes up the hairy creature
Knowing how fast arachnids can run.
Splat! He drives his mashie home -
And scores that elusive hole in one!

Down Memory Lane

Come take a walk my dear one
Down memory lane with me
Cast your mind a way back
When things were fancy free.
Let's step back to the fifties
When big bands used to play
We dressed up in our fancy clothes
And danced the night away.
Bill Haley and his Comets
Played Rock Around the Clock,
The beat was so terrific
We'd dance until we'd drop.
When pointed shoes where all the go
A suit and tie for fellows
And girls wore swirling dresses
Of pink, red and yellows.
The dance halls were enormous
To entertain the crowds
While two bands alternated
With music good and loud.
We'd hold each other closely
That was the way back then
And thank each other nicely
When the dance came to an end.
It seems a long way back now
Such fun it used to be
I'm glad you took a walk back
Down memory lane with me.

If I Should Win the Lottery

Perchance to visit 'gay Paree,'
Ride an elephant on safari,
Sail the seas on an
Ocean-liner,
Dine off the very best
English china,
Own a racehorse -
Maybe three?
Wear the finest
Diamond jewellery,
Dress in the latest
Designer clothes,
Book balcony seats for
All the top shows.
Command a presence
Wherever I go,
Create a well-bred,
Wealthy pose,
Drive a bright red
Lamborghini,
Sip champagne and
Dry martini?
Mine, all of these could
Surely be,
If I should win the lottery,
A major miracle - if they
Should pick it,
For I never buy a
Lottery ticket!

Matilda's Garden

To walk in Matilda's flower garden
At the crack of some early dawn,
Or just on dusk when a silence filled
The eve with drifts of warm;
Or when the dew was on the grass
It was a magic scene -
With crystal-beaded droplets
Spread o'er the leafy green.
When Autumn strewed her rustic lace
Around Matilda's garden bed,
Veined, fallen leaves crunched underfoot
By her cobbled path and shed.
From sparkling webs to silver trails
Where Jack Frost danced till dawn,
Matilda's garden has entranced me
With springtime's nectar'd yawn.
Sweet birdsong in some yonder tree
Filled my days with merriment.
Upon my ear, it was a joy sublime,
Like trills from a sonnet lent.
Long hushed agos, slow afternoons
Spent by a leafy fold,
Where honey bees, so hum-drum
Busily brushed their wings with gold.
While summer's soft green canopies
Exuded a clement breeze,
Cicadas sang ear-piercingly
From the safety of her trees.
When I walk in Matilda's garden
Through ways so old, yet new,
I search among the floral haze
For her favourite bells of blue.

Poor Creature of a Bird

My secateurs clip the dead wood
from the Pom-Pom Tree.
Gnarled bits hit my face;
clipping up, I spy it —
its wings are mattered close to its body;
Caught, grey and wet,
Hanging by a
Single, black thread;
wound round one claw,
Suspended upside-down;
With one eye missing.
Its struggle has shortened
The thread - spun it up,
Entrapping it in the thicket.
The small body, I cut down - burying it
Underneath the Pom-Pom Tree.
Its heritage is the soft grey earth,
of my favourite garden bed.
I wonder now,
as I sew my latest black skirt:
If only I'd gardened yesterday?

My Gal

My very best gal is so well behaved
Her hair is groomed and daily laved.
Such fun we have in our own way,
As we traverse the toils of the day.
As garden gurus in clement weather,
We scratch the soil for weeds together.
Our language-speak is all our own,
A jabberwocky, plain home grown.
Close beside me is my special gal
Her contented note she plies so well
It's a happy tune she likes to share
Expressing her trust with a loving air.
Undercover, she's a Poirot copy-cat,
Sleuthing for that imaginary rat;
And when I pat the bulging Doona -
My gal springs out for breakfast tuna.

Ghostly Touches

Browsing through an old curiosity shop
A sudden cold shiver gave me a shock Startled,
I edged slowly into the adjoining room
Where another eerie shiver came all too soon.
Not able to concentrate on the crafts anymore
I promptly hightailed it from the store.
Feeling uneasy I tried hard to be calm
Lest something or someone did me some harm?
Back at the car where my husband awaited
I related what happened; then he firmly stated:
Two women were slain in that old bluestone place
And never, the killer, did they ever trace!
Now it spooks me to tell of that eerie event
Even to write it or to think what it meant?
For those two separate touches, that ghostly display
Were they warnings to women to stay away?
I've never been back and never would go,
So afraid am I imagining that ghosts may show,
And scare me to death with an apparition;
When I have such a nervous disposition.

Travelling - My Way

I thoroughly enjoyed my China trip
What a journey, with sights galore,
There were bicycles by the millions
Making road crossings quite a chore.
I visited the famous Forbidden City,
Explored pagodas and temples too.
Spent time at the Great Wall of China,
What a fascinating structure to view.
This trip, I travelled on my 'Pat Malone'
And saw people's lifestyle and home,
Their greetings full of grace and charm
I wanted to stay longer to jaw and yarn.
I'm so thankful for a strong construction
For I travel well and don't suffer jet lag,
Or get air sick like some travellers do
And never lose my passport or bag.
I can revisit again any place I like,
At no extra cost or trouble, you see...
I'm an avid, worldly armchair-traveller
Watching travelogues on my tee-vee!

The Pepper Tree

There's a baby in a photograph
taken beneath the pepper tree
and as I scan it more closely
I realise that the babe is me.
Another depicts older children
underneath the pepper tree
all seated around a table
where Gran stands silently.
Now, it's a giant pepper tree
Yet, I can still recall
how Gran did her family's washing
underneath that tree so tall.
Her face grew red from rubbing
it was such an arduous chore
washing soiled butchers' aprons
free of stains and other gore.
The pepper tree was shady
where Gran washed in tubs of tin
she used a wooden scrubbing board
and a copper to boil clothes in.
Gran had no computerised machine
just her poor old reddened hands
which wrung out clothes resolutely
To keep her family spic and span.
The pepper tree kept growing
like the children of the day;
but weeps there like a Willow now,
for they've grown up and gone away.

Bloomers

I've tried to imagine
What the PE Teacher saw
As we bicycled our legs
On the cold wooden floor.
Such Cancan capers
All hips held high
In navy-blue bloomers
We fast pedalled the sky.
Ol' blue-bags were flailing
Round young shapely sticks
Ooh! How blooming awful
Were those elastic-trimmed 'nicks.
I now stop to wonder
How, on some wild windy day
They didn't inflate like balloons
And carry the whole class away!

The Spirit of Progress

The Spirit of the mighty iron-horse
Rides o'er the broad-gauge rails
From Melbourne through to Albury
In a flash of smoky veils.
Just a steam-train apparition
The Spirit of Progress travels on
in the minds of train enthusiasts
Where old steam-trains now belong.
Yet, should you stop to listen,
Cock an ear upon the ground
You might hear the locomotive
Flying fast - Albury bound.
You'd faintly hear the whistle
The hypnotic clickety-clack
Of steel upon steel
Resounding off the track.
You'd see the big wheels turning
And the stocked-up sooty mass
Puffed out dark and murky
From the engine's fiery stack.
Alas, today a diesel runs
O'er new standard gauges
Express through to Sydney
Recording progress in history's pages.
While the old Spirit of Progress
Shunts into cobwebbed railway sidings
Where a semblance of ghostly passengers
Embark on illusory steam-trains ridings.

Bargain Hunter's Safari

Liquorice highway traveller
Miles from my home town
Long distance is no barrier
When I am bargain bound.
City ads are tempting me
Away from my country home
Specials, huge reductions,
To the stocktaking sales I roam.
Bankcard, cash and Myer-card
Are with me all the way
While I check out bargains
And jostle crowds all day.
It's great to shop for bargains
It puts me to the test
And fitness is important
To do my very best.
The pushing and the shoving
The bustle and the rush
My headache's nearly killing me
I need to find some hush.
To be a bargain hunter
You need a lot of nerve
And the patience of a saint
When waiting to be served.
Bags are getting heavy
Feet are getting sore
Blisters now appearing
Can I walk some more?
Bargains keep me going
I'll shop until I drop
When city sales are roaring
I can never stop.
My shoes are really hurting
I cannot walk another inch

Burst blisters I am sporting
There's blood there - that's a cinch.
I limp about on sore feet
All around the store
With my toes all bleeding
'Till I can't shop anymore.
The sales girl's sympathetic
Places new slippers on sore shanks
'Bargain Hunters need old shoes, Dear!'
For this relief - much thanks!

Tree Through History

From small acorns great oak trees grow
Their solid timbers make warships go-
To discover new lands across the seas
And foreign cultures like the Japanese.
To cherry blossoms and Geisha girls
And opium dens with smoky swirls
To bonsai - beautiful stunted trees:
A patient craft of ancient history.
To Egypt and Cleopatra's trial -
Her elongated crafts sailed on the Nile.
To mummified cats and 'tis understood
Where buried in coffins made of wood.
To Holland and the wooden clog
Not recommended for a daily jog
To the land of the cuckoo clock
Where wooden birds keep a timely mock.
To the old bark hut and dugout canoe
And boomerangs that return to you.
To sleepers on the railway line,
And cork stoppers for bottled wine.
To cabinet makers and fancy fret
Where table legs are shapely set.
As the list unfolds about the tree
Its lifespan can be a mystery.
Tho' seeds of renewal replenish again
There are dormancies where no forests remain,
For supply cannot meet man's constant demand,
Outstripping until the last trees stand.

Bangers!

They hang 'em high, hang 'em low
Make 'em thick or thin
Cook 'em in their casings
Or nude without a skin.
Choose red or brown, black or white
Square, twisted, straight or round
Or, linked together in a string
Cheaper buying by the pound.
Kids love sizzled bangers
Slapped 'tween lumps of bread
Smothered in tomato sauce
No left-overs will they shed.
There's Fritz 'n' Strass
And black pudding,
Beef, garlic, pork, 'n' chicken
And tempting gourmet delights
Cold for finger-picking,
You'll find bangers spittin' on a hotplate
Slowly brownin', what a sight,
At any real Aussie barbie
Mainly on a Saturday night!
(Chuck a few prawns on the barbie mate!)

The Nursery

Whale-watchers watch
From Logan's Beach stands
Keeping long vigils
Via binoculars in hands.
Fretting and pacing
The sandy waiting room floor
Anticipating some births
In the nursery harbour.
Expectant father bulls
Wait - spouting off shore
While pregnant cows
Cope alone in labour.
Spy hopping and breaching
And fluking of tails
Heralds the arrival
Of baby Southern Right Whales.
Instincts maternal
With calves at their sides
Mothers suckle their young
With milk that nature provides.
Flippers are flopping
In fun water whacks
As the whales glide slowly
And loll on their backs.
Proud mothers with new calves
Naturally play in the ocean
In a whale-wonderland nursery
Oblivious to the watcher's commotion.

The Door of Inspiration

Repeatedly, I knocked and knocked
at the door of inspiration.
The way was barred to me.
The door closed - padlocked.
The key hidden.
Desperately I tried to get in.
I needed to unlock the door.
If only I could find the key.
Day after day,
I continued to knock and tap,
tap and knock, at the door of inspiration;
seemingly getting nowhere.
I was persistent - never giving in.
No magic wand, or word availed itself to me.
Alone I faced wayward thoughts,
all shrivelled up and small.
No clues came to mind.
Until I took my imaginary slate and white chalk.
I wrote upon it the word 'begin',
which begat 'start'
that begot 'race'
that led to 'win'
which begot 'celebrate'.
'Party' begot 'fun',
'Friends', 'food', 'wine' and 'happiness'.
A jolly jumble of fine words.
Lateral thinking had taken over
snow-balling words together,
making a giant 'word-man'.
Quite unexpectedly I had found the key,
through my lateral thinking.
The way was clear.
I had finally opened the door,
the door of inspiration.

Mondayitis

Monday comes around again
Oh, how I hate it so,
'Cause I feel so blue on Monday
And the week has far to go.
Tuesday it's no better
In fact, I'm kinda low,
'Cause always on a Tuesday
There's a heap of work in tow
Wednesday it's much better
It's to the half way mark,
'Cause always on a Wednesday
'Tis my night out for a lark. Thursday is a great day,
It feels good from the start,
'Cause always on a Thursday
That pay cheque gives me heart.
Friday is a winner -
The best day of the week,
'Cause only on a Friday
That working week I've beat.
Saturday and Sunday
Are just for me alone,
'Cause I do my own thing
Then, wonder where time's flown.
Monday comes around again...

Mirror's Image

There's no narcissism here
For the image factor's not great
To mirror Alice through the looking glass
Would surely be tempting fate.
These eyes grow dim as old I grow
And I bless the powers that be
For the mirror's image softens
So, I miss what others might see.
Oh, vanity used to taunt me
When a girl and in my prime
Since, lags way behind somewhere
Lacklustre in the face of time.
Occasionally, a faint sparkle emerges
Lurking deep within the glass
And tho' these eyes see differently
There hints no touch of class.
Less elegance, less bloom - yet
A distinguished, gentler sight
Borrowed from my gene pool
To view the old age axiom right.

Perpetual Meeting

Daily they meet at the Hopkins River Mouth
Just as the tide runs in and out.
They're always together, by hook or by crook,
A twosome much older than the 'good book'.
They kiss in the morning and again at night,
And run with a passion over sand so bright,
Frolicking and roaming the distant shore,
Steadfastly claiming their daily moor.
They ebb and flow from north to south
And touch each other mouth to mouth,
Then slip away past bridge and shed
Along the furrowed river bed.
At dusk again, returns the tide
Rushing back to the ocean's side.
Silver wavelets abreast the sandy altar,
Where sea and river never falter.
Their merging creates a water eddy
Swelling first, with waves unsteady.
The currents pulling out to sea,
A surge of water running free.
The Hopkins River has snaked on by,
Leaving sandbanks high and dry,
Golden patches await underneath the blue
For that perpetual tide to flux anew.

Mysterious Aliens from Outer Space

We've seen them in movies and comics too
Odd looking creatures unlike me and you.
From outer space, where we've not been
Come superior minds the likes we've not seen.
All appear short, with rough lizard-type skin
Not overweight, in fact most are quite thin.
Dubious in character - except for E.T.,
Whose alien heart-light was so cute to see.
From swollen foreheads to digits slender
It's hard to tell who's who in gender.
Cloned to the very nth degree
Their weird make-up is a mystery.
They visit out planet in saucers that fly
Tho' few will condone the figment of an eye
For captured sightings have been a hoax,
To become the brunt of unbelievers jokes.
So - are aliens around or are they not?
Or are we a curious, imaginative lot?
Whatever the outcome it's plain to see -
Aliens pose problems - paradoxically.

I See My Love

From an ivory tower I watch
Two handsome knights
Vie for my hand
Each has a lance
How cavalier!
Abashed, I see
Their armour
Glisten in sunlight.
They joust for me!
Maiden fair -
With 'Godiva' hair.
Knight one:
Tall, dark, moody.
Knight two:
Bold, red, fiery.
Fearless warriors,
From East,
And West;
Faced in combat.
My lace kerchief
Drops.
Full-thrust, they gallop
Towards each other -
Lances outstretched.
Eyes ablaze -
The horses' nostrils flare.
Hooves pound terra-firma
Like Tom-Toms.
The clash of steel.
My heart races.
Within -
I want them to stop.
Without -
I see my love is red!

The Waterlily

My friend and I walked in the park
One fine summers day
We came across a little pond
And both strolled up that way.
Each spied a waterlily growing
Right in the middle there
So, we thought we'd climb the rock
And pick this beauty - rare.
My friend was plump and I was thin
And both did climb there on.
But as we did the rock broke off
And tumbled us in the pond.
The pond was yabby infested
We screamed and splashed about
And held our derrières tight
Then quickly scampered out.
And the glorious waterlily stayed
With not a petal harmed
While we squelched on home, bedraggled -
All a quiver and alarmed.

Woolgathering

Knit one: How I recall
Little booties, oh so small,
Crafted well, knitted neat,
For my baby's tiny feet.
Knit two, drop some,
Slow and clumsy I've become.
Sweet reverie breaks away,
Woolly thoughts of yesterday.
Picking up the stitches
I knit to the end of the row;
With the visions of booties
Still haunting me so.
Those cream and white socks
My twin babies wore
Knitted lacy, yet deftly,
With much love and adore.
Now, I knit plain squares
Over a garter stitch path;
And then join them together
Making a long Dr Who scarf!

The Junk Drawer

It's a metal mishmash
A square 'drawersome' thing
Cluttered with paraphernalia
And gadgets made of tin.
No one dares to open it -
Their moans are quite clear
For this vision's so awesome
It propagates fear.
There's terror in our kitchen
Real Mutant-Ninja-knives
Dividing and multiplying
In our junk-drawer overnight!
We fear the mutant blades
That slice, stab 'n' bite
And bruise 'n' bleed our pinkies
In junk-drawer finger fights.
There's fear of amputation
From near minus digit-games
As jammed fossicking fingers
Throb with pinkie-pains.
So, when a call for gadgets hails
'Round our clutter prone abode
Sudden deafness becomes a virtue
Lest someone has to rummage through
Our junk-drawer's overload.

Ol' Darlin'

Ol' Darlin' I love you
Tho' I loathe to, I tell
Of a nasty affliction
In short - a bad smell.
I've bed you and fed you
Your house I've kept clean
So, how can I smile
When you're spoiling our scene.
We've played ball together
And done a few tricks
As one we grew up
With no secrets, but
Lately ol' darlin'
You've been a real pest
Oh, how do I deal with
Your filthy ol' breath.
I know of a bright lad
Whose word dear I trust
He washed his pals mouth out
With toothpaste and brush.
Ol' darlin' my sweetie
Some days I just wish
There was sweet smelling dog food
For your halitosis.

Miss Margo's Menu

Let's do lunch Miss Margo said,
And escorted me out to the shed,
The table was set, tin plates askew:
This'll be great for me and you.
She sat me down on a rickety chair,
A bottle of water she offered to share,
Such a to-do, she was eager to please,
And suggested greens with curly leaves.
I nodded yes, that that might just do,
Instead, I was given a floribunda stew
And then cherry pie without a crust,
A recipe that Margo said was a must.
The piece de resistance by Miss Margo,
Was a plate full of frothy, live escargot.
Though deemed a delicacy over in France,
As real garden pests I could take no chance.
Miss Margo was sad and not at all glad,
She hung down her head feeling so bad.
I up-took her passion and making it right,
Drove her to McDonalds to her great delight!

Just Nobody That's Who!

Who left the top off the bottle of sauce?
Why, it was Mr Nobody of course.
Where, oh where is my favourite pen?
Has Mr Nobody got it again?
How did that mud get stuck on the floor?
Who let the dog in through the back door?
Why aren't my scissors in the top drawer?
Where I had left them just as before?
How can things move from that place to this?
Curious isn't it how things go amiss.
Who left chewing gum stuck to the wall?
Why it was nobody, just nobody at all.

The Great Outdoors

I've packed my bag and billy
Tied cork-strings around my hat
My shoes are flat and comfy
I'm ready for the track.
For I'm heading for the Great Outdoors
To see some Aussie bush
Travelling on shanks' pony
Far away from the city's push.
I travel light, there's no overflow
Use a ground-sheet for my bed
A one-man tent to sleep in
And a bluey for my head.
Beneath the Southern Cross I sleep,
There is no grander sight
Those winking eyes of heaven
Are my candles for the night.
Repellent spray is on my face
To stave off the Aussie blight
There's billy tea with gum-leaf
What a Great Outdoor delight!
The crimson glow of morning
Wakes a newer fresher me
To vistas of the ranges
Quite picturesque to see.
And way out west, the koala bear
Nibbles on the eucalyptus leaves
While the kangaroo and emu
Keep the campers company.
The turquoise seas and sandy shores
The red earth and the brown
I'd rather view the Great Outdoors
Than to live-it-up, in town!

My Favourite Place - Internally

There's a favourite place I love to be
And it's all encased in my memory.
I can take it out like a photo book
Anytime I like to have a look.
The pictures are so real to me
For they are in my life eternally.
Friends I've known don't go away
They are within me every day.
Down memory lane I often go
To visit folks, I used to know.
Tho' departed now from this life
I see their faces in the light.
The light that shows me the way
And it pleasures me to go or stay.
For each and every-time I do
I'll find a memory that's new.
To dally here, and to dally there
In peace and quiet without a care.
This is the place I'll fondly be -
It's my thinking part - internally.

The Four Seasons

An inner eye is given wings,
A preview of forthcoming things.
Cerebral images fast portray
The seasons, four, in vast array:
White sandy beaches, colourful clothes.
Swimsuits, surfers, a sun-blocked nose.
Gardens green with grey bosky veils,
Rugs and hampers and cool ginger ales.
Jack Frost mornings and fog filled days,
Gold and rust leafage laying crisp underlays,
A-twisting and turning and gyrating back.
Shuffling together down a wind-beaten track.
Warm cosy fires when winter's wind blows,
Snug woolly socks to warm up blue toes.
Silvery cobwebs, bejewelled with dew,
The man in the moon's pale eerie hue.
Spring breathes a sweet nectar sigh -
Across dormant meadows standing by:
The seasons four, so universal -
Are reborn again - with no rehearsal.

The Gift

I couldn't miss it - for there it was,
standing outside my door - a giant cos!
Its narrow leaves in a curtsied frown,
with outer foliage a fuscous brown.
Around its waist hung a painted note,
with words that made my neighbours gloat.
'You Cad!', I yelled, and burning red,
I wished it was a dream instead!
Jeff Rowe had sent it - my secret wooer.
I wanted to flush it down the sewer.
Instead, I kicked the gift aside,
and reviewed the couplet he did scribe:
LETT-UCE PARTY MISSUS BROWN
WHILE YOUR HUSBAND'S OUT OF TOWN!

Who Owns Matilda?

One hundred years ago
A suicidal, sheep-stealing swaggie
Camped by a billabong;
And waltzed his Matilda.
After three troopers arrested him,
He shouted:
You'll never catch me alive!
He jumped into the billabong.
His ghost can be heard,
If you camp by that billabong -
Singing:
'You'll come a waltzing Matilda
with me!
'Now, the ghosts of origins
Haunt Matilda:
Winton; Warrnambool;
Scotland; Germany,
And -
Banjo Paterson A.B.

Op-Shop Grunges

Lately we're frequenting op-shops
Seeking out old crocheted clobber
Trying on boots with platform soles
And holey jeans that'd horrify Mother.
We forage through racks at the op-shop
And dip into pre-loved clothes
Modelling berets and tight sweaters
To complement our new-look wardrobes.
We're trying hard to look impoverished
Tho' our labels are not cool and neat
We ape the new look with op-shop gear
For grunge fashions never come cheap.
Inspired out of recession and hardship
It's a fashion statement from dismal climes
Designed to be frumpy and a tad dowdy
A fad gleaned from really hard times.
Yes, we're frightfully grunge in our outfits
Our chic berets, boots, dresses and shawls
We're the dinosaurs living animated convention
Wearing old clothes from St. Vincent De Paul's!

Committee Riddle

If a standing committee actually sits
And the sitting committee's vote stands
Will the committee that's sitting and permanently fixed
Stand in address of the seat that's opposing
From the chair of the sitting committee?
And, if that committee which actually stands
Sits again holding onto its seats
Will the chair of the chair, who normally sits
Upturn the sitting committee's seats
Thus, vacating the chair, leaving the sitting
Committee to stand?

The Morry For Me

Sometimes, I'll admire
Cars others acquire –
Still, it's the Morry for me.
She's been good over the years,
Slips smooth through the gears,
Still, it's the Morry for me.
If she's slow off the mark,
Or her motor won't start.
Still, it's the Morry for me.
How they honk and they hoot
While I look in her boot.
Err! Still, it's the Morry for me.
Watch their faces turn grey
As they zoom fast away,
Gulp! Still, it's the Morry for me.
Knockity-knock, splutter, croak,
omitting cloudy blue smoke,
OH! Still, it's the Morry for me.
Yep! They towed her away
On that ominous day,
But still, it's the Morry for me.
Now she's got her new rings
No embarrassing things,
Sure! Still, it's the Morry for me.
Ol' faithful and true,
No other will do,
It's always the Morry for me!

The Aussie Fly

Oh, tell me this 'cause I wonder why
God invented the Aussie fly
It's such a pesky little thing
And carries germs upon its wing.
At picnics, beach and barbecue
That Aussie fly will menace you
Although we're armed with spray in tin
It doesn't stop at anything.
Now the Aussie wave, it came about
From giving flies a mighty clout
And when you see folks waving high
It's likely at the Aussie fly.
The cork-string hat swung to and fro
When bushmen wore it years ago
But sometimes they got mesmerised
From swinging corks before their eyes.
Then beetle (dung) was introduced
But still it seemed of little use
The Chinese look to have them beat
They swat them in their house and street.
Perhaps if we adopt their way
And swat a thousand every day
We'd soon be free to go about
Without that Aussie fly to clout.
They'll even 'free ride' upon your back
For they can see no harm in that
They're such revolting little things
And flit about on transparent wings.
They drop in any time at all
And nearly drive you up the wall
So, grab your swatter, hold it firm
Exterminate this filthy germ.

Just hold it like a tennis bat
And well directed knock 'em flat
Then we can all sing praises high
At eliminating that Aussie fly.

Mirror's Impressions

Waiting...
Ice-picture
In the stillness
Of an empty room
Married...
To rosebuds
Wall-papered
In a floral swoon
Facing...
Subjects all
Never unkind
Only frank
Looking-glass
Silver-backed
If broken
An unlucky prank.
Animated...
Via visual sights
Mirroring, aping
Truthfully.
Image... It isn't me
A replica of Mother
Is what I saw!

My Mother's Flame

Her flame
Of motherhood will not die.
Brightly -
it burns for me,
Warming my heart,
touching my soul;
replaying memories
etched in my mind.
Her flame
Filters through
death's morbid mask,
freely embracing
our good times;
highlighting -
Life!
Laughter!
Cuddles!
Games!
Measured -
not by the hours
nor the days,
but her effervescent
loving ways!
These precious gems, for me,
(her first born),
radiate timelessly
from my mother.

Mr Fix-it

When doors expand, stick or swell
drop 'n' jam or squeak like hell;
or a clownish plaque falls off the wall
to crumble into pieces small...
or an elegant swan of china breaks
and its slender neck decapitates.
There's a handyman we always call
who fixes items large or small.
He'll glue 'n' screw, sand 'n' scrape
and soon enough has things ship-shape,
they're good as new - his time's well spent,
we call his talents - heaven-sent!
Sometimes a lightbulb peters out:
'Help!' Is there a handyman about?
And sure enough - in a trice -
He's fixed it up twice as nice.
A chain of gold has a broken link,
our handyman does twist 'n' twink
untying knots and unravelling line,
Mr Fix-it fixes it - every time!

Tiger-Tim

This rhyme's about a tiger
A cub in black 'n' gold,
Who ran barefoot and swam in creeks
Like any tiger - bold!
But wait - he's not a tiger - real,
Yet somehow, he'd become
A child of nature where he grew up,
Near the town of Casterton.
He roamed the hills 'n' paddocks
Shot rabbits, snakes and fowl,
And hunted all around the traps
Like a tiger on the prowl.
But, that's not how his nickname grew,
And there's no grand tale to be told
It was just because he was wearing
A t-shirt designed in black 'n' gold.
The nickname's stuck some fifty years,
He answers well to Tige, or Tiger-Tim,
While his friends and neighbours
Never know,
If Ronald Leslie's really him?

(Remembering Ronald Leslie Richards aka 'Tige'
1931-1999.)

Twigs

Dried fallen twigs
O'er the apron of earth
Offer fireside warmth
With crackle and mirth.
Make recycled fodder
For nourishment and growth
To budding new trees
And turn acorn into oak.
Strong evergreen twigs
With sap-oozing veins
Produce healthy branches
Quenched by the rains.
Twigs embrace blossoms
And red, golden leaves
That flutter to earth
Kissed by the breeze.
They're the coat hangers of life
The frameworks for bearing
Nature's fabulous treasures
For pleasure and for sharing.

No Mischief Played Around Here

Don't get up to any mischief whilst
Dad and I are away –
you know the rules - obey them:
Mother said one day.
Yeah! Yeah! We know!
There's no need to fuss,
We'll obey the rules,
you can put your trust in us.
No mischief will be played around here,
enjoy yourselves – you've naught to fear!
When at last our folks had gone -
we put our favourite record on,
and nudged each other, gave a wink,
pushed back the chairs and in a twink
rolled up the carpet, kicked out the cat
and with Bill Haley - rock 'n' rolled all night around the flat!

Hypochondria

Health charts lining my doctor's walls
Are directed straight at me
Mentally I spot-check diseases
Pertaining to family history.
Digesting slowly, the printed words
On heart and diet - cholesterol free
To then scan spine and skeleton
And cartilage of the knee.
Bored, I pick up a magazine
And flip o'er a glossy page
To read about a victim
Who lost the fight to AIDS.
A malaise sweeps over me
My stomach's tied in a knot
I'm faint from over-breathing
Nearly hyperventilate on the spot.
Well, I'm incubating a virus
Must be a strain of swine flu,
And I bet I'll get diabetes
Probably ingrown toenails too!
Alas, it'll be me who'll suffer -
Pain from the bladder gall,
So, hurry will ya Doctor -
And give my name a call!

The Hapless Homeless Drifter

Wherever he finds a pad is home
Whether it be a house, poky flat,
Caravan, flimsy two-man tent,
Or timber humpy way outback.
He's quite at home anywhere.
His life's laid-back - non fussed
Uncluttered and unattached,
He's a rolling stone - un-mossed.
He has no ties or tailored suits,
Mobile phones or flashy cars.
He's a loose artillery piece,
Equipped with fur-ball mortars.
He's a contortionist at his caper,
So lithe, so sleek, and laved clean.
He may be of aristocratic lineage;
For his ancestors visited the queen!
He often sleeps beneath the stars,
Or seeks shelter underneath bridges.
He's known to doss in Salvo's bins,
Or old discarded fridges.
But, no one cares about his health,
Or tries to help him on his way.
He's an abandoned, homeless feline,
Adrift, another long and lonely day!

When the Wind Goes Wild

When the wind goes wild
I suffer vexation and bemoan
For the safety of my children
Not made of skin and bone.
Since I have nurtured them
And watched them slowly grow
I have great fear for their lives
Watching them bend and bow.
I tend and batten them down
And pray the wind will dissipate
While the shift through night-time -
Seems an eon to have to wait?
Throughout the windy night I fear
They'll not be sound at dawning.
How I love each one ever so dear;
And the forecast is: storm warning!
Oh, Hyacinth, Daphne, Daisy and Lily,
Sweet Violet and my beautiful Rose.
I hope all of my children will survive;
After the wild wind eventually goes!

A-Sailing on the Water

The water was calm for boating
As we smoothly sailed along,
Moving at a nice steady pace -
Singing an old seafaring song.
Then out-of-the-blue it hit us
This huge sea-monster's fin,
It rolled our small ketch over
And from him we tried to swim.
We struggled a lot in the water
With much flapping of our hands
And righted up the boat's mainsail
Saved, from sinking to the sands.
We did quite a lot of bailing out
To eliminate the fear of waterlog.
Then the wind blew up the foam
And chased away the heavy fog.
Three cheers we yelled in unison:
We have saved our boat today,
From the ravages of the ocean:
We wondered what our dad'd say?
Ahoy, there boys! Out of the tub!
It's time to tie up your sailing boat.
You can sail away some other day,
So now drop anchor with that soap!

Mushroom Madness

Around some mellow mushrooms
On a balmy autumn afternoon
Cattle began foraging hungrily
Hoofing the paddock's bloom
Some sashayed in a circle -
Others skipped along the ground
'Moo-oo!' They cried in unison
It was a weird lowing sound.
The farmer heard the racket
And on his motorbike did hop
One hundred cows were lowing
He could not make them stop.
Wearing earmuffs for protection
He watched how they behaved
Then spied half eaten mushrooms
Where his brindle beasties grazed.
It struck him in an instance -
What made his cows hoof high
For among the mealy mushrooms
Grew some toady old fungi.
This made the farmer wonder:
Did the dish run off with the spoon?
After dishing up funny mushrooms
When the cow jumped over the moon?

Haikus

Baptising the Night

Incandescent orb,
suspended in the dark sky.
A wooer's delight.

Anchor man of night.
Host to bowl-shaped cavities;
besprinkled by light.

Worldly projector,
of heavenly rays and beams,
lambert over night.

Ocean Crafts

Long lacy white crests
embroidered on turquoise waves,
scissored by surfers.

Arsonist

Little match aglow.
So brightly it does flicker.
Cast down - inferno!

Apathy

Who pays attention
to the pink worm on a hook,
drowning in blue water.

* * *

Nescience

The emergency
was born out of ignorance,
for the want of learning.

Barbed

The fragrant red rose
does not reveal the sharp pain,
inflicted by thorns!

 Aftermath

Leaving black torsos,
flames dance merrily along
the dry forest floor!

Growth

Green and proud it stands,
Oak tree stretching up so tall.
Once an acorn small!

Droving Days

Perchance to be like Clancy
Of Snowy River fame -
A rough and tough young drover
With a stock horse - good and game.
Rounding up a mob of scrubbers
And wildly riding out to muster,
O'er mountain top and lower plain
And never seem to take a buster.
The stock whip's crack will tarry
And echo about crags and hills,
While scouting scrub and bushland
Applying well known riding skills.
A pipe-dream takes me droving
O'er lofty hills and saltbush plains
Galloping past the young saplings,
Emulating Clancy with the reins.
The view of rugged mountain tops
And rivers running crystal clear,
While fresh air crisp and biting,
Lashes cool on my face and ears.
Instead - I ride o'er a tarred road
In an old clapped-out motor car,
Polluting up the atmosphere,
Choking back exhaust fumes -
Aaaah!

My First Car Rally 1981 Style

We took Morry on a rally
eighty miles it was to be
on roads that took us all about
to end at Port Fairy.
The cars were all the oldies
of the vintage kind, that go,
looking bright and shiny
they put on quite a show.
We had a special escort
to see us on the road
'cause being very old like,
some of them have slowed.
Drivers wore their favourite caps
with special club badges on -
then off we set together
the line it was quite long.
Chugging through the country
we got a lot of waves,
as people from their houses
stopped and looked amazed.
When we reached Port Fairy
we set up on the green,
all the cars were standing-
orderly, so as to be seen.
People came from everywhere
to look and ooh and aah!
Talking, looking, touching,
the grand parade of cars.
There was vintage and classic
and the post war too,
Morris, Buick, and Pontiac

just to name a few.
And, with many, many others,
show-cased on display,
came out Morry - 'sidewacker'
resplendent in silver grey!

Daffi-Dilli

Daffi O'Dilli
You're certainly not silly
Trumping your trumpet,
willy-nilly
With an edge so frilly.
Your colour is glowing
Such a glorious toning
You're a daffi-delight
A beautiful sight.
Daffi O' Dilli
You're a springtime lily
On a stalk of green
You stand elegant and lean -
A Daffodilli Queen!

Spring's Gowns

Golden needles of sunlight
Slip-stitch my eyes
With colourful threads
In a patchwork surprise.
Reams of pink ribbon
Interlace the earth - brown
Embrace petalled pillows
Appliquéd on the ground.
Blankets of buttercups
Heads bobbing and nodding
Rock 'n' roll with sweet songsters
The blackbird and robin.
Snippets of yellow
Plaited with blue
Embroider nature's patterns
Recycled anew.
A large nectar'd yawn
Breaks over the day
As Spring's debutante blossoms
Put their new gowns on display.

Gardening Heaven

She's leaf-green in summer
A fleur-de-lis
Her kaleidoscopic colours
Perfect potpourri.
She's a botanical treasure
Wearing Autumn's gold and brown.
Wan in Winter's grey bonnet
Until Spring pinks her crown.
But, whether the weather
Is fine or plain drear
It's a gardening heaven
Anytime of the year.
For nature is bountiful
With her fluorescent show
Tho' I'd really much rather -
Her weeds didn't multiply so!

Touching Senses

Oh, hear how he sings
his sweet roundelay;
shrillest song of day.
Woodland bellbird rings,
tolling on his wings,
jubilant and bright
celebrating life,
in sharp ting-a-lings.
The flowers speak too,
with heady perfume
and colourful hue,
to blend with the tune.
bells ring and bells blue;
Spring's birdsong and bloom!

A 'Raining' Republic

G'Day Matilda, it's nice to see...
An' how's the farm an' family?
The weather's crook. The hens won't lay...
'Ave you had water down your way?
The dams dried up, 'ain't got no hay,
El Nino's fault, I hear you say!
I know it's useless to complain...
If only we could 'ave more rain!
This Republicanism's a load of guff,
Will Politicians ever run out of puff?
Does it matter Matilda, who's at the helm...
A-Steerin' us outa this arid realm?
Any'ow luv, it's quite plain to see,
from Australia's colonial history...
bein' hog-tied, most kith an' kin
to mother England's apron string...
the day'd come to walk away -
an' swing our blueys the Aussie way!
Come to think of it Matilda my dear,
we could be free within a few years,
our leader then - tho' I'm hesitant...
will be duly known as the president!
Hang on Matilda, it's occurred to me...
Australia's first president could be a she!
No light relief will it bring to me...
this change in Australia's history,
an' I know it's useless to complain...
but hell, Matilda; we need more rain!

ORDA!

'Let me address the question.'
'I'd like to make this point.'
The issue's raised, the die cast,
ready for question-time in parliament.
Words, often barbed and bated
roll off some speakers' tongues,
in long 'n' fiery oral debates -
delivered with political aplomb.
When senators' polemical voices
swell in cacophonous discord,
the acting president interjects,
Calling, 'Orda! Orda! Orda!'
'Point of orda Mr Speaker,
or the Whip I'll soon employ.
Ask your question Senator,
And, cut that bucketing ploy!'
'Orda!' Cries the President...
'You're out of 'Orda' - all!'
His words fall on deaf ears
At Canberra's parliamentary
Free-for-all!

Pins 'an Things 'an Cotton Reels

I never did like sewing
'twas always such a chore
with pins an' things an' cotton reels
all scattered on the floor.
The cutting out was easy
I seemed to manage that,
but putting it together -
Well, I didn't have the knack.
I'd end up with the front piece
pinned in around the back,
the armhole was big enough
to swing an alley cat.
My zipper wouldn't zip
an' my hem it wasn't straight,
the buttonholes were all too small
an' buttons wouldn't take.
It got me quite bewildered
for the dress might never be?
I even stated decidedly -
that sewing's not for me!
In fact, the dress was made,
albeit, perseverance bearing
from a learned sewing-student,
And moi with muted-swearing!

Stolen Years

Long honey suckled shadows
Steeped deep in memory,
Plucked at the heart stings softly
Stirred momentarily.
Swept, stealth-like into crannies,
Explored windmills of the mind,
Nudged tenderly at doorways
Held fast by Father Time.
Images, bright and beautiful
Through unlocked doors were caught,
Precious, magic pictures
Addressed awakened thought.
Novice, tiny miracles
Twin blessed from above,
Twofold visions recycled,
Conceived with special love.
Reflected in times looking glass
Life's stolen years recalled,
Oh, touched the heart so lightly
Long shadowy fingers all.

Willy-Win

Jumping out of the starting gate
Willy-Win races away are a cracking rate
Ginger-Biscuit clings to the rails -
Behind the main-stream horses' tails.
Willy-Win now sets the pace
With Typhoon-Lin in second place
Under pressure is Silver-Slate
Headed off by Imperial-Mate.
Still running well, is Willy-Win
Pegging back the favourite, Typhoon-Lin
But, Lo, a dark-horse is looming fast
It's Ima-Plodda he's really flying past.
Around the corner, into the straight
The horses bunch and whips gyrate
Ima-Plodda makes loping strides
As hands 'n' heels his jockey rides.
It's neck 'n' neck, three horses race
In a photo-finish, to determine place.
White-faced, I clench my TAB ticket
Wondering, Willy-Won't or Willy-Win it?
Torn confetti hits the lawned surround:
Just a lip between so the photo found,
So close Willy-Was, but then in the end -
Willy-Won't save my WIN betting spend!

Poppies

Poppies mean remembrance
Emblems of our dead
For those who fought for liberty
And suffered wounds and bled
At Flanders - where men fought and died
Back in 1914-18
We pay homage to our fallen boys
At that torrid battle scene
And for all the wars, we wear them
As respect to loved ones lost
While their artificial colour: red,
Depicts real blood spilled - that cost.

Appeasing Appetites

People stand at supermarket shelves
Looking worried and nonplussed.
Their minds cast in a quandary,
Pondering: Which product can I trust?
Will it be the chicken or the veal,
What about salmon in a can?
Maybe a nice mince casserole,
Or a scrumptious steak Diane?
They'll often chat with strangers
Who share in their culinary worries,
And sigh when crossing kidneys off -
A list; deleting crab and curries.
The length of time they'll dally
All for their family's sake -
Selecting but the finest fare
For gourmet meals to make.
So much energy is expended there
To fetch and then to carry -
Over and over and over again
The supermarket aisles they'll tarry.
Then it's home with all the shopping
Which is laden with much food,
And who patiently awaits them?
Their hungry, four - legged brood!

What's Christmas Nanna?

What's Christmas, Nanna?
Well dear, it's faith.
What's faith, Nanna?
Well dear, it's belief.
What's belief, Nanna?
Well dear, it's trust.
What's trust, Nanna?
Well dear, it's faith, belief and hope.
Three things, eh, Nanna?
Well dear, it's complex.
What's complex, Nanna?
Well dear, it's difficult.
What's difficult, Nanna?
CHRISTMAS!

Father Christmas Has to Be Your Dad!

Who said Father Christmas has to be your Dad?
Ours never owned a red suit, or white beard had.
Being a shift-worker at night put him out of business
So the role of Santa was performed by his Missus.
Quickly, she tip-toed all around the house,
Missing the loose boards that squeaked like a mouse.
Mother Claus crept into our bedroom to place,
Those crinkle-wrapped presents that made our hearts race.
We'd peek from under our covers, after she'd gone,
While Mum's familiar rose perfume lingered on.
The night seemed so still, only the noise of a drum
Beating inside our ears, said: Quick morning come!

Traditional Tokens

There's a mail influx and no shortfall,
Textually they say: Greetings all!
Designed to mirror a festive scene,
With mistletoe berries and holly, green.
It's a postie's annual, errant chore,
Delivering daily to each box or door,
From me to you and you to me -
Going to and fro intermittently.
Special cards gather about the house,
A motionless lot - quiet as a mouse.
Their words of cheer and sentiment -
Bring smiles and incite merriment.
Larger cards greet us musically,
With verses waxing on lyrically,
Performing tunes, we love to hear:
Jingle Bells and The Midnight Clear.
Lines may thin from year to year,
Some shy away, others disappear.
Friendships formed in novel places,
Help fill a void of empty spaces.
As the weeks roll by, battalions grow,
Cardboard soldiers stand in a row,
Guarding seasonal wishes on display;
Traditional tokens of Christmas Day.

Keying In

Ol' St Nick was on his way
Computer surfing in his sleigh
Going through the lists on screen
Scanning for chimneys unforeseen.
Some were round, some were square
Some were derelict and in disrepair.
Tall or squat Nick had to view -
The ins and outs of pots and flue.
Tight sometimes their fit would be
And tho' Nick dieted regularly -
He often wished that he had a key
To make a more accessible entry.
Prancer and Rudolph knew the score
And could trot and stop at any door,
Instead of precarious rooftop highs
Affecting hips and scraping thighs.
So, the elves designed a special key
That Nick could use repeatedly -
For keying in on Christmas Night,
No chimneys posed a barren sight.
Now the 'chimney-less' needn't fret,
'Cause Ol' St Nick will be on deck
With designer key to turn the locks
To fill those empty Christmas socks.

The Scent of Christmas

The fibre optic Christmas Tree
Has lights that excite visually
A chameleon in deep purple hues
Changing back to greenish-blues.
As I view this ultra-modern wonder
Brown study makes me stop and ponder
The simpler times when twigs of green
Permeated the Christmas scene.
Glittering shells, some painted red
Macaroni strung on coloured thread.
Paper chains which trailed forever
All glued and stapled up together.
Stars and moons made out of dough
Hung with holly and a bright red bow.
Streamers were cut from paper crepe
With fringes of cellophane to decorate.
Balloons all round would sway and flop
With a silver paper star perched on top.
A pine aroma filtered through the air
Evoking us Christmas was almost there.
The heavenly scent of the Christmas Tree
Seemed to exude a penchant for charity,
Awakening the good spirits, love and care,
Heralding in Christmas as a time to share.

Santa's Aussie Dress Code

Santa Claus has cut his beard.
It was so long, so white, so weird.
He's stashed his suit, so fiery red,
And lost the sock upon his head.
That gear's too hot for Aussie climes,
And after crossing international lines,
He'd notched up miles and different times,
Felt cold then hot, he'd read the signs.
He knew his dress code was passé,
And didn't suit the Aussie way,
So, his gear took on a khaki hue,
Now he looks a Santa that's true blue!
He wears flip-flops on his swollen feet,
And short shorts to cool his sweaty seat.
A cork-strung hat to swing and sway,
And keep the pesky Aussie flies at bay.
Six boomers pull his laden sleigh,
To rev them up he shouts 'G'day!'
They freedom-ride o'er rooftops high,
Listen fast and you may hear him cry:
'Ho! Ho! Ho! Merry Christmas! Ho! Ho! Ho!'

Online Santa

Santa lost his mobile phone
Such a quandary he was in.
He rifled through his Santa sacks
And through his deer's food bin.
Mother Claus grew testy
And threw her arms up in dismay:
How could you be so careless,
You should be on your way!
Santa frowned and paced about
Mother thought he'd have a fit,
The sleigh was hitched and ready
Deer were champing at the bit.
Rudolf's nose was turning pale
And Prancer pawed the ground.
'Oh, my deers,' cried Santa
'My Elf-line's not around!'
A tintinnabulation came
From inside Rudolf's throat,
Jingle bells was playing low -
Santa thought his deer had bloat.
The reindeer gave a snort and cough
And out flew the mobile phone -
Louder rang the jingling bells;
The elves were phoning home!
Santa's helpers packed the sleigh
With toys and gifts galore -
Then set off with a Ho-Ho- Ho!
For that was Santa's roar!
Christmas Eve passed merrily,
The delivery date was met
And Santa chastised Rudolf
For his mobile eating debt.
Now, Santa's into laptop mode

Deterring mobile-eating deer,
He gets emails on the internet
And can be found ONLINE all year!

Christmas Haikus

Ye Ol' Christmas
Tree Askew and covered in dust
Allergy hazard!

Ye Ol' Christmas Tree
Lay in a pile of rubbish
Fossickers recycle!

Ye Ol' Christmas Tree
Candelabra centre piece
dust busted festoon!

Now You're Christmas Ready

Well, are you Christmas ready?
Have you begun to decorate the tree?
Or hang up the Christmas stockings
On the mantelpiece near the chimney.
Are all the presents wrapped and tied?
And placed neatly beneath the tree-
Where chameleon lights a-blinking
Make a picturesque sight to see.
Have your Noel cards been posted?
Or your Facebook greetings entered
To those who prefer online greets-
While others are snail-mail centred.
So, the turkey's stuffed and basted
And roast-ready for everyone to eat.
While the pudding's boiling steadily
You've made a brandy custard treat.
Lo, should your guests arrive early
You simply fill their glasses - tall -
With lots of cool champagne bubbles
And turn up the new TV on the wall.
Now that you are Christmas ready -
Lots of duck face selfies will appear.
In lieu of a mistletoe/kissing-bough
You have a broccoli-bough this year!

The Brightest Star

Like moths drawn towards a light,
Three wise men sought out a sight:
Where the Son of God was born
They travelled all night until dawn.
Guided via the brightest star,
The men had trekked so very far,
Arriving at a specific stable door
To view the baby that Mary bore.
Bearing frankincense and myrrh
And a basket full of gifts and fur,
The sages silently knelt to pray:
For peace on Earth that holy day.
Those Christian blessings still remain,
For all who worship in Christ's name.
The faithful pray for peace on earth,
As did three wise men at Jesus' birth.
As those gifts were offered at the start,
With a simple faith and a merry heart,
Our prayers will deepen and increase
Until the whole world can live in peace.

Cool Alert!

They're not average backyard chooks
Nor pelicans in children's story books,
Or penguins wearing black bow-ties
And not wise owls with rounded eyes.
They came in pairs each year in spring
And could those divas sweetly sing!
They'd harmonise in the morning sun
Until their frenzied fossicking was done.
Such special blackbirds - every one,
Who ruled backyards from sun to sun.
Always alert and with watchful eyes
They'd search for naughty gals or guys,
Then pitch their song to Ol' St Nick
And name the ones who'd get the flick.
Timed children, who were wise to this,
Held wagging tongues until Christmas
Believing they would get to have a say
And dibs cool gifts from St Nick's sleigh.
Cool kids were in, un-cools were out,
To be cool was best without a doubt.
The little black book, an unfair guise,
For ticks or crosses was no surprise.
'Twas toe-the-line for good not bad.
Lest un-cools were left an empty bag?
Christmas dawned clear and bright,
And not a single blackbird was in sight,
They'd finished work as St Nick's scouts
And no one knew of their whereabouts?
Mother had cursed them with a frown,
She'd spied their calling cards around:
Dirty 'dobbers' she was heard to say,
That's so un-cool on Christmas Day!

Good Intentions

It takes courage to be resolute
To be steadfast until the end
To walk the straight and narrow
And not be weak and bend.
With a New Year just beginning
While just a babe in arms
It's not easy to build character,
Quelling those tempting qualms.
Yet, I made my resolutions
With bright eyes and bushy tail
And hopeful heart and stoic mind
Into a brand-New Year, I sail.
Alas, February's arrived already
And I haven't lost that weight
But next month I will lose it
Soon I'll be a trendy size eight.
Easter, oh, my sweet tooth:
It's death by chocolate - I fear!
My New Year's resolution - well,
There's still practically a year?
August winds are so chilly
I must eat up to stay warm.
A few more little kilograms
Will keep me cosy in a storm.
Christmas and plum pudding,
Now I'm overweight I fear -
But I trust my good intentions
Will serve me well - this year!

The Colours of Australia

The colours of Australia
Unfurl as gold and green
Wattle trees and gum-trees
A unique Australian scene.
The people of Australia
White, yellow, black, brown.
A melting pot of colours
From near and far abound.
The colours of Australia
Built from the old gold-rush
And grey sheep a-grazing
In meadows green and lush.
The colours of Australia
Deep red in Mallee towns.
Beneath the Southern Cross
A turquoise sea surrounds
The colours of Australia
With a chameleon Uluru
Its rusty-orange colours
A tourist's snap-shot view
The two flags of Australia
Coloured: Blue, red and white
And black, yellow and red:
The colours of Australia unite!

Summer Nights

Hot summer nights. How to stay cool?
Suffering night sweats, that is the rule.
Radio listener with talk-back all night,
Topics are cool, handy hints and the like.
Some folks are lucky, they have a cool room,
With ducted cooling, that must be a boon.
My pedestal fan dips and then sways
Backwards and forwards, slowly it plays.
Forward is nice, I feel a soft breeze,
Backwards I don't and sweat bubbles bead.
I toss and I turn, and sleep just won't come
Hot summer nights are rarely much fun!
Once on a hot night I slept out in the yard
The house overheated; sleeping was hard.
I dragged my mattress straight off my bed
And curled up on it, just near the shed.
But, like copies like, and oh, what a bore;
My neighbour slept out and began to snore!
All through that night he kept me awake
As I swatted mosquitos off my face!

Knowledge Bumps

Knowledge bumps. What are they?
Are they something handed down
Or does one have to earn them –
Like a boxing champion's crown?
Are knowledge bumps like measles
That spread and multiply -
Or simply one-off eruptions
Red and shiny like a sty?
Do swollen heads induce
Knowledge Bumps
And how do highbrows' rate
Will students grow larger
Knowledge bumps
After each passed exam they take?
And what of an explanation -
About this unusual lump of mind -
That's feasible and reasonable
And not difficult to define?
For I never grew a knowledge bump
And tho' I'm told that they do exist.
My partner grew one on his wrist -
A ganglion - knowledge cyst?

Summer Moon Rising

True love's like a summer moon
Joyous with golden light
Swathed in pure magic
Its aura glowing bright.
Love that's true fills the soul
And warms the heart with gold
Lifting flagging spirits
With arms that hug and hold.
Huddled 'neath the summer moon
Large chunks of heaven smile
As lovers whisper sweet-nothings
And away their secrets while.

Missing Missives

Whatever happened to letters,
Words written on paper with pen?
Correspondence to each other,
Whatever has happened to them?
I used to look forward to mail
A letterbox check didn't fail.
Email's the way mail's sent today,
Very few missives are posted away.
It's electronic touch screen jobs,
In lieu of messy black ink blobs.
Whatever happened to Xmas cards
Handwritten by buddies and bards?
Now it's a form printed spiel
Unspectacularly typed, no zeal,
Waxed with newsy tidbits galore.
Printed out by the dozen or more.
It's of handwritten letters I'm fond,
No Shakespearian inky frond,
Nor a thumbnail dipped in tar,
Or a telegram sent from afar.
Move over new cyber generation,
Crank up the trusty Vespa, Jason,
This dinosaur is so letterbox worn,
Seeking a letter via postie this morn.

No Worries!

If I could put worry in a pocket
And push it way, way down
I'd lose it in a second
And clear away my frown.
I wouldn't want to pull it out
Not even for awhile
Since it's been contained
I smile instead of frown.
A worry should be buried
Whatever way you can
For worry brings on stress
And makes you feel undone.
So if I put worry in my pocket
My life will surely better be
Relieved of any awful cares
And in turn make a better me!

The Heat Is On

The heat is on, nine days straight
When will hot weather dissipate?
Keeping cool is my only notion
And drinking any cooling potion.
Clearing out a room of clutter
Not one expletive did I mutter.
Newsletters I found in a neat pile.
With printed verses honed in style.
Poetry! Created by names I know,
With verses that did ebb and flow.
The heat is on, nine days straight
How lucky I found poems that rate.
Perusing poems thru' and thru'.
Verses, rhyme, a couplets coup
Such a friendly poets' corner find,
Now cool I am, at least in mind.
Climate Change is here to stay
So I'll just read hot times away,
Going back thru' times now gone
Willing a change to come along!

Necessity, the Mother of Invention

Once threepence held stockings up
When suspender buttons pinged
And daubs of red nail polish
Stopped a ladder reaching shins.
Pantyhose were helpful
Should a car's fan belt break
Slipped around the pulleys
Still, the trip to town you'd make.
Chewing gum was a great plugger
For stopping up holes in plasterboard
Pegs made handy bag-sealers
Where no jars or tins were stored.
But, a favourite bit of inventiveness
Must go to my granddad's whim -
He used to brush his grey moustache
With black boot-polish from a tin.
Those tales of bread and dripping
Made my tummy feel quite awful
Folks ate this with salt and pepper
Mostly, enjoying every morsel.
Commonplace inventiveness
Sprung from harder yesteryears
Tho' today's throw-away society
Has more waste - than frugality to fear.

Grandma Laughingly Said...

With six and two ha'pennies
tucked tightly in my hands,
face to face in the hallway
I encountered my old gran.
'What have you there, child?'
Grandma asked, with a smirk,
as my double-fisted hands
dived underneath my shirt.
'Don't act so coy, dear.
Let Gran have a sticky beak,'
and slowly I unfisted my fingers
so Gran could take a peek.
In less than half a moment
my coins went spinning through the air
while Gran chuckled loudly
at her quick, underhanded flair.
The eight-up trapeze act
came tumbling back down
and like Gran's sense of humour
twisted round and around.
And, as I crawled about the floor
fast collecting all of my money -
Grandma laughingly said...
'A girl and her money are soon parted, Honey!'

The Greatest Gift

The only gift that lasts and lasts
Cannot be bought with cash or card.
It's so elusive, can't be gift-wrapped
Foolish to try because it's too hard.
The only gift that lasts and lasts
Is given from the tenderest heart,
With lots of affection thrown in
This gift is hard to pull apart.
The only gift that lasts and lasts
Is made from a very special mould.
It's core is mainly heart and soul
The perfect gift for young and old.
The only gift that lasts and lasts
Can be free and as gentle as a dove,
Or strong with a faith everlasting
And the most perfect gift is: LOVE!

World Without End

A soothsayer said today the world will end
Such predictions have been cited before
By futuristics with a crystal ball trend,
Psalm quoting with mixed up folklore.
My preference being a world without end
For negative foretelling is becoming a bore.
So I'll keep to the faith, hold fast the dream,
And continue to live and follow God's scheme.

Feathered Friends

Each morning, come what may,
He toddles down a track
To a cherry tree, denuded,
In his garden, down the back.
He swings a wee bag of food
Held loosely at his side,
As tentatively he measures
Each hobbled, arthritic stride.
Looking up at his tree, so bare,
He spies naught on branch or wing;
Just a silence in the frosty air
And no sign of anything.
Carefully, he fills a bowl
With breadcrumbs and fruit,
And any left-over morsels
The old man thinks will suit.
Still; He watches furtively,
As one by one they come
To feed at his cherry tree
Every famished, feathered one.
Content, he listens quietly,
As all the birds begin to sing;
Their trilling voices united
In a thankful carolling!

Pelican

Of all the birds there are to see
The pelican provokes much curiosity
For he has a comic grace and charm
The way he swans on lakes so calm.
Tho' awkward on a river bank
He wobbles like a broken tank,
But when he sets off into flight
He makes a most majestic sight.
Before his flight path has begun
He takes a long and lumbered run
Across the water to gain some height
Then soars aloft like a feathered kite.
His accentuated pale pink beak -
Takes centre stage in marsh or creek
Whilst greedily he'll scoop and pan -
His beak holds more than his belly can.

Joys of Travelling

The steam-train trip was very long
My girlish legs began to fidget,
For I was only fourteen years
And classed then as a midget.
Kerang, it seemed so far away,
Yet I kept my flagging spirits high
By listening to the engine talk:
It hissed out steam or gave a sigh.
The wheels resounded off the track:
Clickety-click, clackety-clack.
They took me far away from home,
I felt grown-up but so alone.
The carriage shifted to-and-fro
There was a distance far to go,
When from my seat I spied a scene
Of puffy clouds, like in a dream.
The smoke took shape across the sky,
I saw a horse's tail float by,
An ice-cream cone, a party hat;
I'm sure I saw a white fluffy cat!
As I rode along the railway line
These visions gave me pleasure time,
Cloud-watching all the smoky haze
Gleaned solely from my steam-train days.

Mementos of Gran

Seed cake and Anzac biscuits
filled my grandma's cake tins.
Large kettles used to boil
on her wood-stove's back ends.
Her kitchen clock tick-tocked
with its gold pendulum,
and her kerosene lanterns
Brightened every room.
She had wash basins and jugs,
a claw-footed bath;
open fireplaces with coals
that sparked on her hearth.
Milk covers, edged with beads
to keep blowflies away,
and water pumped from a well,
which was part of her day.
Her varnished pianola
was played with her feet,
by pushing two pedals
up and down to the beat.
Yet time cannot erase
her brand of perfume,
or the sight of chamber pots
beneath beds in bedrooms.
I still like to remember
Gran's square-cut glass beads,
for they sparkled like diamonds,
so, I used to believe.
These mementos of Gran
I've tried hard to recall,
but she was quite old then,
while I was quite small.

One Good Turn

Grandpa grunted with effort
Quaintly cursing, his face grew red:
'Well, bally-bust-up-to-it!'
Quite plain and loud he said.
He widened his arthritic hands
His face grimaced with pain
Like King Bruce and the spider,
He tried and he tried again.
He applied more concentration
And strained so hard to win.
When a bout of frustration hit
He fought on; would not give in.
Might did not come easily,
What little strength has waned,
And try as hard as he might
His efforts were all in vain.
Hard; stuck the golden disc.
Reluctantly, he passed it to Ma.
He offered up a 'Well Done',
As she twisted the lid off the jar.

My Favourite Movie

The star in my favourite movie
is a classic curiosity.
There's magic in her red shoes
and her name is Dorothy.
Her companion dog is Toto.
He's always at her side,
until a nightmare twister,
leaves them no place to hide.
Eventually, they're transported
to the Emerald Land of Oz,
after following down a brick road -
that's yellow - because, because.
They meet some oddball characters,
who have some disabilities:
One has no brain; one has no heart;
and the third is courage-free.
Down the yellow brick road
the plot gets thick,
after some scary encounters
with the wicked old witch.
But the good witch saves them,
and the old hag fries -
From the wave of a wand
before Dorothy's eyes.
Then they discover the wizard's a fraud
and feeling homesick and very bored,
Dorothy makes a wish to go on home,
where Toto is treated to a juicy bone!

The Mother Hen

Comfy she looks on her nest of straw
Captured contentment to be sure.
Mother Hen sits in a pregnant pose
Warming her eggs and boney toes.
Grace exudes her calm demeanour
With plumage white, none are cleaner,
Her crimson comb a crescent match.
Serene, she awaits her chicks to hatch.
She turns her head away from me -
In a pose of paused simplicity.
Tho' oblivious what surrounds her lot
On a cupboard door is made to squat.
My favourite bird sits in painted bliss
A daily treat I would never try to miss.
My feathered friend sits so prettily-
Poised in a work of art for all to see.

Senior Citizens - Mushing On

Senior Citizens have the happy knack
of quietly going thru' their paces...
delivering meals to people's homes
while wearing broad smiles on their faces.
After a chat they sally on forth -
lest hot meals cool off in their car
for waiting elsewhere with bated breath
there's another meal-on-wheels customer.
Their actions are not crippled by strikes
for freely they give of their precious time
working together as a well-oiled machine
sustenance - ferrying, so others may dine.
Senior Citizens volunteer to be useful -
to assist those who have special needs.
Like St Bernards, trekking thru' snow,
mushing on, and doing good deeds.

A Mother's Hands

A mother's hands
feed,
burp,
change
and clean.
Dry,
fold,
powder
and cream.
Pat,
tie,
pin
and peel.
Hug,
hold,
lift
and wheel.
Caress,
calm,
wipe
a tear.
Scold,
correct,
banish
a fear.
Gather,
provide,
mix
and share.
Comfort,
juggle,
guide
and rear.

What a day!

It started out quite badly
From the moment I woke up.
First, I bumped my saucer
And spilled tea from my cup.
Then I stubbed my toe and swore,
It helped to quell the pain,
For it hurt like the Dickens
Then it smarted all over again.
The milk boiled over on the stove
And the cat threw up on the mat.
So, the calendar I quickly checked:
Friday the thirteenth – fancy that?
The milkman left one carton less
And the paper boy – it wasn't hard
Excelled himself, and with biceps large
Tossed our paper into next door's yard.
Then as I sorted out the dirty clothes
To place in my washing machine,
I found a bill I thought was paid
Stuck fast in a pocket of Sue's jeans.
It was outstanding – in the red;
My face aped this and then I read:
"Final Notice – note the pay by date
Or the debt collector is your fate!"
Just then I got some woeful news
Via fax machine in the other room,
That Aunty Bess – my favourite aunt –
Was dying; and likely pretty soon.
The world's gone mad – I was to think
And feeling wan – not in the pink,
Poured out a scotch and was to say.
'Well, here's to me. Boy! What a day!'

She's my Inspiration

Fresh inspiration struck me today
For I was smelling the roses and vowed:
I will soon be my old self again!
I was thinking aloud, as if in a cloud.
Alas, little Miss Four mistook my remark,
But you'll still read me rhymes, Gran?
I smiled at her sweet, innocent words,
Yes, darling child, as often as I can.
Her favourite verse from a poet of old
Is Jack Frost nibbling fingers and toes…
He paints wonderful pictures in the night
And the last line is a chorus of ho, ho's!
But I feel truly blessed by her request:
Won't you read me some of your rhymes?
Then she picked up my book, took a quick look,
And pointing, said: 'Read this one on the lines.'
Well, I keep it short for my little Miss Four,
Her attention span can be easily jarred,
She loves to hear rhymes most any old time
She's my inspiration and p'haps a new bard.

Can I Mum?

Can I have a biscuit, Mum?
Can I, can I, pleeaase?
No dear, it's dinner time.
Go wash your hands and knees.
Can I have a chocky bar?
Can I, can I, pleeaase?
No pet, believe me - It'll spoil your tea!
Can I have some cake, Mum?
Can I, can I, pleeaase?
You'll be eating shortly.
Go and feed your guppies!
Can I have a cola, Mum?
Can I, can I, pleeaase?
You can wait till meal time
For roast lamb and veggies.
Can I have an ap - (ple)?
Aw! There's gravy on my sleeve!
Can I have some peace child?
Can I, can I, pleeaase?

Mothers-To-Be

Peanut butter, pickles and ice-cream,
watermelons in July,
a hankering for the unusual
mothers-to-be want to try.
Taste buds drastically altered,
demanding expensive delights,
unpredictable fads and cravings
for 'ungetatable' food at midnight.
Oh, devil-may-care in their fetish,
they'd kill to abate their desire,
and woe betide any partner
who relishes quelling their fire.
A father-to-be is often nonplussed.
Simply, he can't understand
how a ravenous, insatiable craving
so despicable can get out of hand.
Calmly, he tends all her bidding,
no time to sit, stare or mope.
Often a prospective father
feels useless and a dope.
Mothers-to-be are neurotic,
their behaviour a little irate.
They curse when they can't see their tootsies
when their tummies begin to inflate.
Then they'll often accuse their poor partner
for their body - rotund, out of shape.
Call them names - animals, demons,
an unfair advantage to take.
'You did this to me - you piranha!
Keep away - you're the one I despise!
Oh no, wait! Pass the pickle jar, honey.'
Then the men see the love in their eyes!

How The Library Changed his Life

Crippled with arthritis,
And emphysema too
Bob made his monthly pilgrimage
With jeep-in-tow to view
Books at the local library,
Which he was addicted to.
They gave him some light relief
From the boredom he well knew.
He'd escape from dire realities:
Shortness of breath and cough,
To browse through the westerns,
And seek out a mystery with plot.
He'd always choose the larger print,
It was so much easier to read,
And satisfied with his collection
He'd then load up his jeep and leave.
Yes, the library had changed his life,
Albeit, if only for a little while...
The reading gave him hope again,
While the freedom made him smile.
He solved many crimes with Sherlock Holmes,
And rode the cowboy's dusty trail.
The library opened up a new world for him,
When his health began to fail.

Not Alone

On a bleak and brumal August night
Gordon and his mate, Jim, went fishing.
They sat at one end of an old wooden bridge,
Two die-hard fishermen, casting and wishing.
The bridge was undisturbed and quiet,
And as the river snaked on by, dark and mysterious,
Gordon and Jim began smoking and reminiscing
Over past fishing adventures, albeit, inglorious.
They got a pull or two, but there were no big fish.
Tiddlers sucked at their bait, none where biting.
Jim had just reeled in and was about to re-bait,
When Gordon said, 'Look, there's lightening!'
'A storm's more 'n' likely,' Jim declared, sagely.
Then he thought he saw a flicker of a lantern light,
And whispered, 'We're not alone on the bridge tonight.'
Slowly, Jim edged his way towards the eerie sight.
As Jim crept unsteadily along the creaking old bridge
A wraithlike cloud enveloped the slippery span.
And an eerie cry and a splash was heard
With the clattering of a chain or a tin can
'Are-y-you ok?' Gordon, croaked.
Hearing no reply, he set off after Jim,
And groping through the mist, bumped into him.
'Arrrh!' Screamed Jim, deducing ghosts can swim.
Gordon laughed, 'Call Ghostbusters, mate.
Nah! Make that Powercor.
There's a power pole sparking.'
A lightning strike - no more!

Wednesday's Percussion

Each Wednesday morn'
Just after dawn
War erupts down my street
As the garbo's bin-up a treat.
There's a thunderous roar
From a mechanical bore
A hissing and squeaking of brakes.
Startled, the whole neighbourhood awakes.
They start with a BANG
A CLANG-a-lang-lang
Then a THUD and a SLAP
A WACK-WACK.
A Percussion begins
With a drum-out on bins
And the reverberations
Of emptied out tins.
Those garbage bins ring
And rhythmically sing
C'latter-c'lang-
A-lang-a-bing-bang!

My Most Endearing Characteristic

What's my most endearing characteristic?
Well, to answer I'm taken to task!
For to romance would be boastful
And too much in the limelight bask.
After mulling the whole matter over
In the far reaches of my brain
I was struck with honest appraisal
Tho' I mustn't appear pretentious or vain.
And, while not aiming to be egotistical,
That's definitely not my style,
I concede to an endearment most natural
So contagious it makes people smile.
Then this question I posed to my family
'What is my most loveable quirk?'
And after a short pause they answered -
'It's your laughter, they said with a smirk!'

Lemon Toaster

Blasting off its silver pad
Another blackened scud-missile
Spearheaded towards the ceiling
Peaking - to nose dive.
Untrackable - it exploded
And dispersed.
Pieces of junk
Hit the floor
In a sooty fall-out.
Spewed from a volcanic machine
The mattered under - crunch
Created by an over-zealous 'lemon' toaster
Proved big on power - mean on munch!

The Proof of The Pudding...

It hung about in abeyance
Clothed in unbleached calico
Confined to homely quarters
Tightly bound with string and bow.
Its rotund bottom was heated
To bubble, bounce and balloon
Until almost ready to burst
From its soggy cloth cocoon.
It had developed and matured
And once defrocked and plain
Made a desirable Christmas treat
Enhanced by the magic of flame.
When it took to centre stage
It brightened up so many faces
As the flames danced and died
Spreading joy to people's places.
The holly that once adorned its head
Lay on the tablecloth in bits
All the bowls were emptied out
And naught was left - not even pips.

Winter

Winter's blowing at my door
I'm prepared for it once more.
Got my hottie, got my rug,
And hot toddy in a mug.
Warm I'll be in woolly socks,
Got some tissues in a box;
Just in case the sniffles flow,
Or sneezes burst or explode.
Still - I know I'm pretty fit,
When I come to ponder it.
It's rare I get a nasty cold -
Even though I'm nudging old.
Endure I must that flu injection,
Hoping to stave off an infection.
Rain and sleet won't bother me
Warm as toast, I'll snuggly be,
Tucked up in my feathery fold,
I won't succumb to winter's cold.
Nah! Wintertime won't bother me,
Like bears, I hibernate - literally!

A Moment in Time

Cradled in the crook
Of my elbow
As snug as a bug
His newness
Burns my cornea
Selfies win praises on Facebook
Picture perfect
Together
The new
And the old
Greeting all
My first
Great Grandchild
And me
Locked -
In a special moment
In time!

Cat 'E Comes

Softly, he comes to me
Showing purr-fect love
Singing his song of contentment
As gentle as a dove.
Expressing trust and loyalty
He's serene and debonair
And in his aristocratic way
Extends a paw to share.
He sings for me, his favourite song
It's a 'murr-notonous' little ditty
His chant unfolds, to hypnotise
And relax this feline kitty.
Cat 'e comes, and cat 'e goes
Yet, curled up on my knee, humming
He seems purr-fectly settled
While his motor is still running!

Good Listeners

Oft I spy a smothered yawn
Well-practiced and well metered
Behind watery eyes or dainty hands
As my tales and poems are greeted.
I prattle on - ignoring yawns
To delve and veer and drone
Delivering of my latest work
Quite eager to make known.
At first my listeners are willing
To show attentiveness
But, locked between voice and paper
They soon lose consciousness.
I catch their awkward straining
All sleepy-eyed and lost
In a more-or-less vacant-pose
But I carry on at any cost.
Until a yawn and bored smile
Across their faces stretch -
'Like a cuppa, Mum?' asks one,
When I hadn't finished yet!
Good listeners are hard to find
They're scares as hen's teeth here
Still, I've got my micro cassette
recorder
A good listener - 'till the batteries
go queer!

Spring

The warm fertile earth cracks open -
ANIMATED
ushers green up to blue.
UNFURLS
with life's promise
WASHES
in gentle rain
SHIMMERS
anointed by sun
NASCENT
on centre stage
CURTSYS
to the wind
BLOSSOMS
The show has begun.

The Pen - Shaper of Words

From my scribbled text
To enlightened minds
Or, well metered rhymes
On indelible lines.
I speak out loud
Without a voice
Help polish prose
The writer's choice.
I'm a love-letter specialist
In long hand scrawl
Using phrases, commas,
And punctuations, all.
A short hand Master,
All scripts written tight
And writer of odes,
With poetic insight.
I'm a powerful tool
Mightier than swords,
A modern-day quill -
the pen - shaper of words
Outmoded by some
With internet and such
A scribe's written note
Has that personal touch.

Look Upon the Rose

Have you stopped to see the rose,
Or look up at the sky,
No, you were just too busy
Then another day slipped by.

 You push and shove to get about
Life is too short you say,
Perhaps you'll make it shorter still
In living it this way.

 Try courtesy, it doesn't hurt
For you'll be old one day,
A little smile, a kind 'hello'
And then be on your way.

 Some kindness to your fellow man
He's very much like you,
It's little things in life that count,
Small gestures that you do.

 To see a smile upon a face
Is reward enough 'tis true,
For beauty is around us all
So, stop and look anew.

 Old folks they are slowing down,
But they are people too,
Who see the beauty in the rose
And in young folk like you.

 Slow down awhile to see the rose,
The beauty of its bloom
Hold fast the memories of a day
Let not the days consume.

Fond memories are made for those,
Who like to stop awhile
To see the beauty of the rose,
And make their lives worthwhile.

About the Author

Shirley Richards

Six decades of correspondence to family and friends (some now 'de-perched') set the writing bug in motion for Shirley when she left the city to run a hairdressing business in a rural Victorian town at 19. These days she messages those still on terra firma via the internet. Snail mail and stamps have been left in the past for the most part.

Two poetry driven highlights have been a media release about flies, and an autographed tea towel from Mr Sam Twining of the world-famous English Tea Company saw her poem about teabags published in his private poetry collection.

These were stepping stones to writing more poetic ditties which were published in newspapers and anthologies (along with a few short stories). She has published two poetry books. She has also won prizes for some of her work.

Now at 84 years of age Shirley is going digital with her first eBook, after a running a popular page on Facebook as a way to find a new audience for her art.

Shirley lives on the South-West Coast of Victoria, Australia with her cat, Leo, with whom she shares a birthday. She's a mother of three, grandmother of two, and great-grandmother of one. She's still writing poetry, and never misses writing a new Christmas poem to send out every year.